Vanilla

by Janet Hazen
illustrations by Susan Gross

CHRONICLE BOOKS

SAN FRANCISCO

Dedication:

This book is dedicated to my brother Bruce, whose love and passion for vanilla exceeds even his addiction to chocolate. It does appear to be a genetic predilection, but I must admit, Bruce was "on" to vanilla long before I was. Imagine...

I would like to thank my editor, Carolyn Krebs, for her diligent work on my four books in this series, and for her keen eye for detail.

Thanks to Bill LeBlond and all those at Chronicle Books who helped create a series of very handsome cookbooks.

Text copyright © 1995 by Janet Hazen.
Illustrations copyright © 1995 by Susan Gross.
Book Design: Marianne Mitten

Library of Congress Cataloging-in-Publication Data
Hazen, Janet.
  Vanilla / by Janet Hazen ; illustrations by Susan Gross.
    p.   cm.
  Includes index.
  ISBN 0-8118-0254-X
  1. Cookery (Vanilla) 2. Vanilla. I. Title.
  TX819.V35H39 1995   94-16139
  641.6'382--dc20   CIP

Printed in Hong Kong.
Distributed in Canada by Raincoast Books, 112 East Third Ave., Vancouver, B.C. V5T 1C8

10 9 8 7 6 5 4 3 2 1

Chronicle Books
275 Fifth Street
San Francisco, CA 94103

Table of Contents

Introduction

Vanilla conjures images of freshly baked cookies emerging from the oven, steaming hot and gooey; of luscious rich ice cream flecked with thousands of flavorful, tiny black dots; and of golden egg custards, smooth and creamy. Indeed, it is difficult to resist vanilla's sweet, elusive scent and flavor; at once exotic, familiar, and comforting, it has been adored by young and old for hundreds of years.

The warm and inviting flavor of vanilla is intricate and complex. Those who appreciate subtle, refined flavors have embraced the essence with a passion that rivals that of the common chocoholic. Stimulating, intoxicating and provocative to the palate, vanilla has staying power where chocolate rapidly makes its statement and departs, much like a passionate but short-lived love affair.

Vanilla is the secret ingredient that adds punch to many of our favorite foods. After all, vanilla ice cream devoid of vanilla would simply be sweet cream, *crème brûlée* is barely recognizable without a healthy dose of the bean, and chocolate brownies baked without a splash of extract taste incomplete. I use vanilla in a wide variety of sweet and savory dishes: the plump beans in fresh or dried fruit compotes, vanilla vinegar in meat stews and vinaigrettes, and vanilla extract and vanilla sugar in lemonade and in most baked goods.

Vanilla comes from a rare and exotic species of yellow orchid native to Mexico. The exact origins of the use of vanilla beans for culinary and medicinal purposes is unclear, but historians believe that tribes living in Southeastern Mexico may have first utilized the bean at least one thousand years ago. The Aztec emperor Montezuma (1502-1520) promoted the use of vanilla long before the rest of the world. The Aztecs used the vanilla pod to flavor their bitter chocolate drinks and in herbal medicinal tonics. Even then, vanilla pods were a precious and rare commodity; they were used to pay tribute to the emperor and as a form of currency.

When the Spanish explorer Hernando Cortez landed in Mexico around 1518, he found that the Aztecs treated this magical bean with great respect. Called *tlilxochitl*, "black flower," by the Aztecs, and *vainilla*, from the Latin *vagina*, or "sheath," by the Spaniards, the pod also captured the interest of Cortez. He returned to Europe with bags overflowing not only with gold, silver, and chocolate, but with vanilla as well. The prized vanilla pod was immediately embraced by Europeans, who loved its distinctive flavor in baked goods and regarded it as an aphrodisiac. The Spanish also mixed the vanilla beans with chocolate, but eventually abandoned the bean for the more accessible and reasonably priced cinnamon for pairing with chocolate. The French continued to use the vanilla bean as a primary flavoring agent in confections and ices as well as in perfumes and tobacco. Today, vanilla is still favored throughout Europe, but its popularity has also spread to all corners of the world.

American Thomas Jefferson first encountered the bean during a trip to France. Upon returning to America in 1789, he missed its warm, enticing flavor, so he wrote to William Short, an American diplomat in Paris, and asked him to send fifty pods of vanilla for use in his kitchen. Between Jefferson's enthusiasm for the bean and the inevitable diffusion of food products from Europe to the United States, vanilla fast became a popular staple in American kitchens. By the 1800s, "tincture of vanilla," or vanilla extract, began to appear in the United States with regularity and was quickly adopted as an easy, swift way to add vanilla flavor to baked goods and beverages. Using the fresh, whole bean was apparently too much work for the impatient American cook, and as a result, for culinary uses the popularity of vanilla extract grew more than that of the vanilla pod and beans. Vanilla extract is now a basic ingredient found in kitchens throughout America, indispensable for using in a variety of baked goods and desserts.

Along with saffron, vanilla is one of the most expensive and precious spices in the world. There are many laborious steps in the production of vanilla, from the pollination of the vines to the careful and delicate care of each pod. Although the vines are now easily grown in many tropical parts of the world, until the early 1800s, only vines in Mexico produced vanilla beans. At that time it was discovered (several people have been credited with this) that a bee indigenous to Mexico was responsible for pollinating the country's vanilla orchid flowers. Once the bees' method of infusing each flower with pollen was understood, a new program of hand-pollination was put into practice with great success. Vanilla plantations began to appear in hot, tropical areas throughout Central America, the West Indies, Indonesia, Reunion, Tahiti, the South Pacific, the islands of Comoro, and Madagascar.

Of the thirty-five thousand species in the *Orchidaceae* family (the largest family of flowering plants) there are only three species of vanilla orchid that produce edible fruit. A healthy vanilla orchid vine will produce close to a thousand blossoms, but only pollinated blossoms develop into pods. Small greenish flowers appear in clusters of approximately twenty per leaf axil. The flowers open for a few precious hours during the morning, when bees, birds, or human hands carry the pollen from one flower to the next. Unpollinated blossoms drop by nightfall, but fertilized blooms develop fruits within four to six weeks. At that time, excess buds, flowers, or pods are removed to give the plant all the energy it needs to produce healthy, robust vanilla pods.

The green pods grow close to twelve inches in length and take about eight or nine months to fully mature before they are harvested. At this point the beans are firm, thick, plump, and yellow-green in color, with golden brown tips. The beans are then harvested by hand and taken to be cured either in commercial curing houses or by hand in the countryside.

Ironically, neither the orchid nor the vanilla pod have an aroma; it is only after curing that the plump pod develops any scent. I will never forget my first and only venture into a vanilla orchard on the island of Bora Bora, a small island close to Tahiti in the South Pacific. I entered the grounds fully expecting to be instantly seduced by the overwhelming aroma of vanilla. I also anticipated a grand view of thousands of ink black vanilla pods hanging from lush green vines. I was surprised when I realized the tiny, green, string bean–like pods *were* the vanilla, devoid of the intoxicating aroma I so adored.

There are a number of different methods for curing vanilla beans; each region favors a different technique. In Madagascar, the Comoro Islands, and Reunion, the curing procedure begins by blanching the pods in boiling hot water to halt the ripening process. The pods are then laid in the hot sun to dry and cure. They are alternately wrapped in blankets to sweat, then returned to the sun to dry.

This curing process is repeated for two to four weeks, or until the pods are dark brown and pliable. In Mexico, after cultivation the beans are immediately stored in sheds until they begin to shrivel—about three to four days. They are then left on blankets to dry in the sun. In Java, the pods are partially dried and then lightly smoked over smoldering fires to finish the drying process. As a result, these beans have a subtle, smokey flavor not found in other vanilla beans. After curing, all beans are sorted according to quality, wrapped and labeled, and sold to appropriate dealers or wholesalers.

There are several varieties of vanilla pods widely available today. Currently most popular with professional cooks and chefs is the short, fat Tahitian bean, which is meaty, rich, aromatic, sweet, and emphatically vanilla in taste. "Bourbon" vanilla beans and beans from the Comoro Islands and Madagascar are of high quality and very plentiful. They are moist, plump, and quite greasy on the exterior. Their high volume of seeds and mellow flavor make this variety a good source of vanilla flavor. Mexican beans, which are high in moisture, very popular, and generally less expensive, are also a good choice. Each vanilla pod contains approximately ninety thousand beans or seeds; even the pods that contain relatively few beans are still loaded with the intense essence of vanilla.

Foods prepared with fresh vanilla have an unmistakable background of thousands of tiny black dots—the vanilla beans. These flavor-packed seeds or beans provide an intense taste of pure vanilla as well as a delightful, slightly crunchy texture.

Pure vanilla extract, an alcohol-based, clear brown liquid flavored by vanilla beans, has an intense, richly fragrant quality. Imitation vanilla extract is usually lighter in color, thinner, sweeter, and less aromatic than pure versions, and it often has a very bitter, unpleasant aftertaste. Once your palate has experienced the unadulterated flavor of genuine vanilla, you will probably want to discard imitation extracts or low-quality beans. When looking for fresh pods, choose those that are plump, pliable, juicy, and aromatic, and avoid beans that are dry, brittle, light in color, and devoid of aroma.

Included in this collection of sweet and savory recipes are basic formulas for vanilla extract, sugar, vinegar, and syrup. Almost all of the sweet recipes call for vanilla extract and vanilla sugar; if you don't want to use the homemade versions, simply substitute pure commercial vanilla extract and use plain granulated sugar. The recipes that call for vanilla vinegar and/or syrup will lack that extra dimension of vanilla flavor if the ingredient is deleted, but champagne or white wine vinegar could be substituted for the vanilla vinegar, and, in a pinch, corn syrup mixed with a dash of extract could be used in place of the vanilla syrup.

Vanilla is a spice that seems to scream dessert. Certainly most baked goods would be flat and one-dimensional without a splash of vanilla extract or the addition of the perfumed, paste-like vanilla beans. But why limit the use of the precious potion and sumptuous beans to sweet dishes? In addition to some traditional and new desserts and confections, I have included several interesting and unusual savory dishes that incorporate fresh vanilla beans for flavor accents.

I enjoy challenging the palate as much as I do educating and pleasing it, and when presented with unfamiliar but inviting flavor combinations, I discover additional delight and amusement in cooking and eating. I hope you can use this collection of recipes as inspiration for creating many more uses for the beloved and versatile vanilla pod.

Vanilla is added to such cosmetics as face powders, lotions, and bath oils,
and is an essential ingredient in many perfumes and colognes.

INTRODUCTION

11

A Vanilla Compendium

Purchasing Vanilla Pods and Extracts

Vanilla comes in a variety of forms: vanilla pods, vanilla extract, vanilla powder, vanilla sugar, and vanilla oil. This book provides recipes using vanilla pods to make your own vanilla extract, vanilla sugar, vanilla vinegar, and vanilla syrup. Good quality vanilla extracts also can be purchased in any grocery store, specialty food shop, or natural food store, but vanilla sugar, vinegar, and syrup are not usually sold commercially and therefore must be prepared at home.

Whole vanilla pods are often called "beans," so you may have to ask for vanilla beans rather than pods when purchasing your vanilla. Either way, the pods should be plump, soft, slightly greasy, and very aromatic. Avoid buying pods that are dry, hard, and brittle as they are old and have little flavor. Pods are best stored in tightly sealed, thick plastic bags, therefore those sold singly in plastic tubes or stored in a jar and sold in bulk are often stale. Instead, look for pods sold in small quantities in airtight plastic bags. If you should buy a hard vanilla pod by accident, immerse it in hot water until soft or store in vodka or rum until pliable. The length of time will depend on how old and brittle the pod.

When buying vanilla extract, be sure the label says "pure vanilla extract," and avoid imitation vanilla flavoring. The alcohol content must be at least 35 percent, and it should contain no sugar, caramel color, or preservatives. Extracts that do contain additives are required by law to state the contents, although they are not obliged to state the amount of sugar added to the extract.

Storing Vanilla Pods and Extract

I suggest storing vanilla pods in a tightly sealed plastic bag in a cool, dark place. If fresh when purchased, whole pods can last for three or four months if stored properly. Alternatively, store whole pods in vodka or rum or in a jar of granulated sugar. Although pods stored in sugar will remain drier and more pure in flavor than those stored in liquid, at the same time they stand the chance of excessively drying out sooner than those stored in vodka. Conversely, small amounts of liquor will most likely seep into pods stored in vodka or rum, and while this method prolongs the succulent, pliable properties of the vanilla pod, it also introduces liquor into the product. If this is an issue, you may want to consider keeping pods in sugar if storing for extended periods of time. Otherwise, I prefer the plastic bag method as it keeps the product pure and unadulterated.

Vanilla extract will last for up to seven or eight months if stored in a tightly sealed bottle and kept in a cool, dark place. Once opened, vanilla extract begins to loose its potency because it is comprised mostly of alcohol, which eventually evaporates along with the flavor.

Vanilla sugar and vanilla vinegar will keep indefinitely because both sugar and vinegar are excellent preservatives. If the pod is left in the vinegar, the vinegar will continue to improve with age up to one year. Likewise, if pods are covered with granulated sugar, the sugar will become more and more intensely flavored over time.

Preparing Vanilla Pods for Cooking

To prepare the pods for cooking, remove the tiny black beans from the pod by splitting the pod lengthwise using a very sharp paring knife. Separate the two halves and flatten slightly, cut sides up. Using the dull side of a knife, run the blade along the cut side of the pod, scraping the beans from the interior as you go. Run the blade over the pod once again to remove any beans that remain. Both the beans and the pod are now ready to use in recipes.

Many recipes in this book call for both the pod and the beans while others use the beans only. In recipes that use both, bear in mind it's the long, cylindrical and inedible pod that must be removed before serving or eating a dish, not the hundreds of tiny black beans!

Cooking with Vanilla

Beans and pods are usually added to foods at the beginning of cooking so that the flavors have plenty of time to marry and meld. The pods are especially good in long-cooking dishes that benefit from extra vanilla flavor, and in dishes in which it is convenient and easy to remove them at the end of cooking. As with many flavoring agents, vanilla beans loose their punch if cooked too long, but when cooked just the right amount of time, they have an opportunity to release their essential oils and intense flavor. The recipes in this book use vanilla in such a way as to fully exploit the natural flavors and qualities of the fresh bean.

Vanilla extract carries the flavor of pure vanilla in an alcohol base, thus when added to foods that will eventually be cooked, the alcohol evaporates, leaving only the essence of vanilla. Except in baked goods, extract is usually added toward the end of cooking or just before serving since the flavor dissipates when heated over a long period of time. Extracts are most often used in baked goods, sauces, and in dishes whose appearance would be marred by the addition of fresh beans, which look like tiny black dots. Still, vanilla beans are a fine substitute for vanilla extract in most cases. Generally speaking, the flavor intensity of one vanilla pod approximates one tablespoon of pure vanilla extract.

AN IMPORTANT NOTE: A prudent amount of pure vanilla extract adds flavor and a minimal amount of color to a dish, but too much imparts a bitter, unpleasant taste. Therefore, more isn't always better when it comes to using vanilla extract. The advantage of using fresh vanilla pods is that an abundance of beans simply adds more intense vanilla flavor without a bitter or acrid aftertaste.

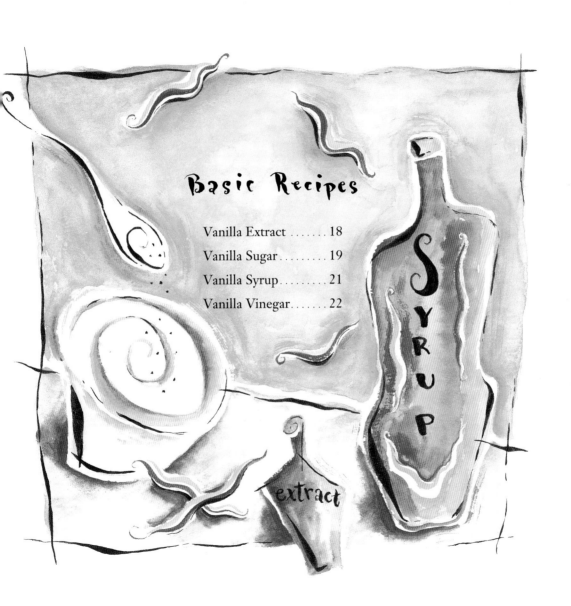

Basic Recipes

Vanilla Extract

Good-quality vanilla extract takes only minutes to make in your own kitchen and its flavor is unsurpassed. Use this homemade extract as you would any other commercial variety.

8 vanilla pods, split lengthwise and
*   beans removed*
1 quart vodka

Place the vanilla beans and pods in a 1-quart bottle with a lid. Add the vodka and mix well. Store, covered, in a cool, dark place for at least 2 months before using. The extract will become stronger as it sits and can be stored at room temperature for up to 1 year.

Makes 1 quart.

To make a spice mixture for mulled wine or apple cider, combine six split vanilla pods, four cinnamon sticks, eight cardamom pods, six whole cloves, two star anise, and the zest from one orange. Mix well and wrap in a double layer of cheesecloth. Simmer the spice package in three quarts of wine or apple cider for one and a half hours or until the fragrance fills the air.

Vanilla Sugar

Once you acquire a taste for vanilla, this sugar will become indispensable. Use the vanilla sugar in any recipe that calls for both sugar and vanilla, as well as in hot coffee or sprinkled on buttered toast. When I have leftover vanilla pods, I add them to the container of vanilla sugar. I have incorporated this flavorful sugar in most of the sweet recipes in this collection.

4 vanilla pods, split lengthwise and beans removed
6 cups granulated sugar

Place vanilla beans in a large bowl. Add ¼ cup of the sugar and mix well. (You may want to use your fingers to thoroughly mix the beans with the sugar as the beans are moist and stick together.) Add the remaining sugar and mix well, distributing the beans throughout the sugar. Add the pods and transfer to a storage container, cover, and store at room temperature indefinitely. Use as you would regular granulated sugar in baked goods and desserts.

Makes 6 cups.

Vanilla is one of the most common flavors used in the preparation of pharmaceuticals. Cherry and orange come to mind when we think of cough syrups, but many liquid medicines as well as vitamins and other pills have a base flavor or coating of vanilla.

Vanilla Syrup

I thought I invented vanilla syrup a few years ago, when I was experimenting with ginger and fruit syrups, but I soon discovered that the mixture has been around for decades, if not centuries. Use this heavenly syrup for desserts; stirred into hot teas, coffee or mixed drinks; and drizzled over fruit, yogurt, pancakes, waffles, or ice cream. One of my favorite dessert recipes in this book—Vanilla Cream Tartlets with Blueberries (page 51)—calls for this syrup.

2 quarts water
3 vanilla pods, split lengthwise and beans removed
6 cups sugar
1½ tablespoons Vanilla Extract (page 18)

Place the water and vanilla beans and pods in a heavy-bottomed, 4-quart saucepan. Bring to a boil over high heat. Cook over high heat for 30 minutes, scraping the sides of the pan often. Add the sugar and return to a boil. Cook over high heat for 45 minutes or until the mixture is thick and syrupy, stirring often to prevent the mixture from boiling over. Add the vanilla extract and mix well. Remove from the heat and cool slightly.

Strain the mixture through a fine wire sieve. Cool to room temperature. When cool, transfer to a glass bottle or plastic container, cover tightly, and store in a cool, dry place for up to several months. If the syrup begins to crystallize over time, reheat over a low flame until liquid and smooth.

Makes about 2 cups.

To help remove the scent of fish or other pungent food odors from your hands, wash your hands with hot water and soap and then rub vigorously with vanilla extract. Rinse with cold water and enjoy your wonderfully scented hands.

Vanilla Vinegar

Use this delightful mixture when you want to soften the vinegar flavor in dressings or vinaigrettes. Or add a splash to soups, stews, pasta dishes, or recipes made with cream when a slightly acidic character is desired, or if you wish to brighten the flavors.

2 cups champagne or white wine vinegar
1 vanilla pod, split lengthwise and beans removed

Place the vinegar in a wide-mouth, nonreactive container. Add the vanilla beans and pods; mix well. Cover tightly and store at room temperature for at least 2 weeks before using. Remove the beans and transfer to a dark, glass bottle with a tight-fitting lid. The vinegar will keep indefinitely if stored in a cool, dark place. Use as you would any other vinegar.

Makes 2 cups.

There are over fifty species of the vanilla orchid, but due to the root disease, inferior quality, and low output of beans common to many, only three have been used commercially: Vanilla planifolia, Vanilla pompona, *and* Vanilla tahitensis.

Beverages

Indian Spiced Coffee with Vanilla

Similar to the classic Indian spiced tea drink, this recipe uses strong brewed coffee rather than black tea for its liquid base. This is a good drink for those who enjoy the robust flavors of Indian spices, dark roast coffee—and vanilla!

3 cups strong dark roast coffee (such as French or Italian roast)
½ cup water
2 vanilla pods, split lengthwise and beans removed
1 teaspoon each ground cinnamon and nutmeg
½ teaspoon ground cardamom
1 star anise
3 cloves
3 to 4 tablespoons Vanilla Sugar (page 19)

Place the coffee, water, vanilla pods and beans, cinnamon, nutmeg, cardamom, anise, and cloves in a 4-quart, heavy-bottomed saucepan. Bring to a boil over high heat. Reduce the heat to moderately low and simmer for 45 minutes. Strain the mixture and add the vanilla sugar. Mix well and serve hot or over ice.

Makes 2 to 3 servings.

Vanillin, the distinctive flavoring agent produced by the vanilla pod, is also found naturally in the bark of the ponderosa pine and a few other coniferous trees. Vanillin can also be found in the sapwood of certain firs.

Mexican Chocolate with Vanilla

Whole milk combined with vanilla, sweet spices, and just a touch of chocolate make this drink both rich and filling. Serve this spicy beverage for dessert after a Latin meal, for a cold weather breakfast drink, or as an afternoon beverage along with Mexican pastries.

1½ quarts whole milk
3 vanilla pods, split lengthwise and beans removed
1 tablespoon ground cinnamon
1 teaspoon each ground mace, nutmeg, and allspice
½ cup Vanilla Sugar (page 19)
4 ounces bittersweet chocolate, finely chopped

Place the milk, vanilla beans and pods, spices, and vanilla sugar in a heavy-bottomed saucepan. Bring to a boil over moderately low heat, stirring frequently. Simmer for 10 minutes, stirring frequently. Remove the vanilla pods and discard. Add the chocolate and stir until dissolved. Whirl in a blender until thick and frothy. Pour into mugs or cups and serve immediately.

Makes 4 to 6 servings.

Vanilla vines reach their maximum production around their eighth year,
but when properly managed and cared for, can produce vanilla pods
for several years longer.

Raspberry-Orange-Vanilla Cocktails

Rosy red in color and bursting with the flavors of summer, this refreshing vanilla-scented cocktail is sure to please all. If serving without the vodka, you may want to thin it with a little ice water.

2 vanilla pods, split lengthwise and beans removed
2 cups fresh orange juice
1 cup raspberries
6 jiggers (9 ounces) vodka
10 ice cubes, crushed

Place the vanilla beans, orange juice, and raspberries in a blender. Purée until smooth. Strain through a fine wire sieve. Return to the blender and add the vodka and ice. Purée until the ice is finely crushed and the mixture is smooth. Pour into chilled glasses and serve immediately.

Makes 4 servings.

Vanilla pods fresh from the vine are plump, green, and resemble a green bean. The pods range in length from six to twelve inches and are ready to be picked after about nine months on the vine.

Savory Dishes

Beet Salad with Two Citruses and Vanilla

Using a combination of small yellow beets and pink or red beets makes this a stunning vegetable salad. I prefer the more complex, slightly sweet flavor of Meyer lemons in the vinaigrette, but any fresh lemon will be fine for this recipe.

8 medium or 16 baby beets, trimmed
1 vanilla pod, split lengthwise and beans removed
⅓ cup olive oil
2 tablespoons Meyer lemon juice
1 tablespoon sherry vinegar
1 tablespoon tangerine zest
1 tablespoon Meyer lemon zest
Salt and pepper, to taste
1 bulb fennel, tough outer leaves discarded, thinly sliced

Place the beets in a medium saucepan and cover with water. Bring to a boil over high heat. Reduce the heat to moderate and cook for 40 to 45 minutes or until they are tender when pierced with a fork. Drain well and cool to room temperature. When cool enough to handle, remove the skins and the "tails." Cut into sixths if using medium-sized beets, and leave whole or halve if using baby beets. Place in a serving bowl.

To make the vinaigrette: Place the vanilla beans and olive oil in a small bowl and mix well. Slowly add the lemon juice, whisking constantly to make a smooth emulsion. Add the sherry vinegar and mix well. Add the tangerine and lemon zest, season with salt and pepper, and mix well.

Add the fennel to the beets, drizzle with the vinaigrette, and mix gently. Adjust the seasonings and serve at room temperature or slightly chilled.

Makes 4 servings.

Endive and Grapefruit Salad with Vanilla Mussels

Light and subtle, this healthful salad makes an excellent warm-weather supper. The vanilla-infused mussels, pleasantly bitter endive, and sweet grapefruit make a winning flavor trio, and are best complemented with a buttery chardonnay wine.

To cut the grapefruit into "fillets," or sections, use a sharp paring knife to slice between the thin membrane and the flesh of each section. Each wedge of fruit should be free of the thin membrane on either side.

1 pound (about 30) small mussels (buy only mussels with closed shells)
¼ cup kosher or coarse sea salt
2 cups water
1 cup dry white wine
1 vanilla pod, split lengthwise and beans removed
3 cloves garlic, minced
2 medium heads endive
3 tablespoons extra-virgin olive oil, plus additional oil for drizzling
1 tablespoon Vanilla Vinegar (page 22)
Salt and pepper, to taste
1 or 2 large grapefruits, peeled and cut into 12 sections
⅓ cup coarsely chopped toasted walnuts
Freshly cracked black pepper

Scrub the mussels with a stiff wire brush to remove any sand or grit. Place the mussels in a large bowl with the salt. Cover with cold water and let sit at cool room temperature for 1 hour or in the refrigerator for 2 hours. Drain well and rinse with fresh cold water. Set aside until needed.

Place the 2 cups water, wine, vanilla beans, and garlic in a large, shallow saucepan. Bring to a boil over high heat. Reduce the heat to moderately low and simmer for 10 minutes. Add the mussels, cover, and simmer for 3 minutes or until most of the shells have opened. Remove all the mussels that have opened and place in a colander. Cook the remaining mussels for 1 additional minute. Remove any opened mussels and add to the colander; discard any that have not opened. When cool enough to handle, remove the meat from the shells and place in a medium bowl; set aside until needed. Discard the shells.

Remove 12 of the large, outer leaves from the heads of endive. Set aside until ready to use. Cut the remaining endive across each head into ¼-inch slices. Add the sliced endive to the mussels along with the olive oil and vanilla vinegar; mix well and season with salt and pepper.

To serve the salad: Arrange three leaves of endive in a fan shape at the corner of each plate. Place a section of grapefruit inside each leaf. In the center of each plate, place a small mound of the endive-mussel salad. Garnish with the walnuts and drizzle with more olive oil, if desired, and freshly cracked black pepper.

Makes 4 servings.

*Vanilla is the second most expensive commercial plant to grow,
harvest, and produce—only saffron is more expensive.*

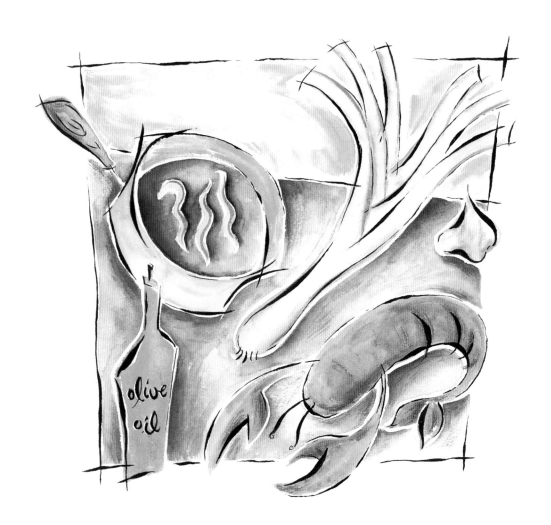

Lobster Ravioli with Sage Brown Butter

Decidedly rich and extravagant, this sumptuous pasta recipe is surprisingly simple to prepare and cook. A few prime ingredients such as fresh lobster, browned butter, and, of course, vanilla work together to make this an unforgettable and unique dish.

I prefer to use prepared *su mai* skins for this particular recipe, but if you can't find this variety of packaged Asian wrappers, use square wonton or the thicker, round potsticker skins instead. Both can be found in any Asian food store and in the produce section of most grocery stores.

RAVIOLI FILLING:
2 large leeks, tough outer leaves discarded, white part only
2 cloves garlic, minced
1 vanilla pod, split lengthwise and beans removed
3 tablespoons olive oil
1 tablespoon unsalted butter
2 cups finely chopped uncooked lobster meat
Dash cayenne pepper
Salt and pepper, to taste

3 rounded tablespoons cornstarch
⅓ cup cold water
One 16-ounce package su mai *wrappers (60 wrappers)*
4 ounces (1 stick) unsalted butter
¼ cup fresh sage chiffonade (cut into very fine ribbons)
3 to 4 ounces imported Parmesan cheese, grated

To make the filling: Halve the leeks lengthwise. Cut crosswise into thin half-moon shapes and transfer to a large bowl; fill with cold water. Swish the leeks around, separating the leaves and removing any dirt or sand. Remove the leeks from the water (do not dump the water out with the leeks). Drain well in a colander.

In a large sauté pan, cook the leeks, garlic, and vanilla beans in the olive oil and butter over high heat for 10 minutes, stirring frequently. Remove from the heat and cool slightly. Add the lobster meat, cayenne pepper, salt, and pepper; mix well. Cool mixture before making the ravioli.

To assemble the ravioli: Make a slurry by combining the cornstarch in the water; mix well. Arrange 10 *su mai* skins on a flat work surface. Brush each skin with the slurry, taking care to spread the slurry all the way to the outside edges. Using 2 rounded teaspoons per ravioli, place a mound of the filling in the centers of 5 of the skins. Immediately lay a second skin over the filling and bottom skin of each, matching the outer edges. Begin pressing the skins together from the filling out toward the edges, taking care to squeeze out any air trapped in the ravioli. When all the air has been removed, seal the last area around the edge and place on a baking sheet (see NOTE). Make the remaining ravioli in this fashion.

To cook the ravioli: Bring 6 quarts of salted water to a boil in an 8-quart pot. Add the ravioli and return to a boil. Immediately reduce the heat to moderately high, and cook for 2 to 3 minutes or until the ravioli float to the surface and the wrappers are tender. Remove with a strainer and immediately place on a large platter or individual plates. (Do not pour the hot water and ravioli into a colander as you would ordinary pasta—these delicate packets are very tender and must be lifted from the cooking water.)

Heat the butter in a small saucepan over moderately high heat for 1 to 2 minutes. When the butter begins to brown and smell nutty, remove from the heat and add the sage; mix well. Immediately drizzle over the ravioli, garnish with grated Parmesan cheese, and serve.

NOTE: The ravioli can be placed on baking sheets in a single layer, placed in the freezer, and frozen solid at this point. When thoroughly frozen, store in plastic bags or wrap in tin foil and freeze for up to 3 months. Take care not to break the thin, delicate edges of the ravioli when wrapping.

Makes 26 ravioli (4 to 6 servings).

*The Aztecs thought vanilla a potent aphrodisiac, a belief perpetuated by the Spanish after vanilla
was introduced to Europe via early Spanish explorers.*

Smoked Chicken Risotto with Vanilla

Vanilla beans add a pleasing background flavor to this hearty Italian rice dish. The subtle essence of vanilla combines well with the smokey flavor of the chicken and tender strands of Swiss chard. Serve a crisp white wine with this unusual and satisfying entrée.

You can find whole smoked chickens and smoked chicken breasts in upscale butcher shops or stores that specialize in poultry. Most full-service grocery stores and delicatessens also carry some kind of smoked chicken. If you cannot find smoked chicken, substitute a good-quality smoked turkey.

1 bunch Swiss chard, trimmed and cut into ¼-inch-wide strips (about 6 cups uncooked)
4 tablespoons (½ stick) unsalted butter
3 tablespoons olive oil
2 medium onions, cut into small dice
4 cloves garlic, minced
2 vanilla pods, split lengthwise and beans removed
2 teaspoons dried rosemary
2½ cups arborio rice
8 to 9 cups chicken stock or low-sodium chicken broth
4 cups chopped smoked chicken meat
Salt and pepper, to taste
¼ pound Parmesan cheese, grated

Wash the Swiss chard and drain well. Drop into a pot of salted boiling water for 10 seconds. Remove immediately and plunge into ice water. Drain well and set aside until ready to use (you should have about 2 cups).

In a heavy-bottomed, 8-quart saucepan, melt the butter in the olive oil over moderate heat. Add the onions and cook for 15 minutes, stirring occasionally. Add the garlic, vanilla beans, rosemary, and arborio rice and cook 3 or 4 minutes, stirring constantly.

Add 2 cups of the chicken stock and bring to a boil over high heat. Reduce the heat to moderate and cook for 5 to 7 minutes or until the liquid has been absorbed. Add 3 more cups of chicken stock and cook, stirring occasionally, for 20 to 22 minutes, or until the liquid has been absorbed. Add the smoked chicken and 3 more cups of chicken stock. Cook, stirring occasionally, until all the liquid has been absorbed and the rice is tender but not mushy, 10 to 13 minutes. (If the rice is still too firm, add 1 more cup of stock and cook until it has evaporated.) Add the Swiss chard, mix well, and season with salt and pepper. Garnish with some of the cheese and serve immediately; pass the remaining cheese separately.

Makes 8 servings.

Chicken Mole with Vanilla

Traditionally made only with Mexican chocolate, not vanilla, this version of the classic Mexican poultry dish is enhanced with the discreet but delicious flavor of vanilla beans *and* bittersweet chocolate. Dusky-flavored chilies, sweet and savory spices, and bright vanilla vinegar also lend their flavors to make this a deep, rich, and very complex-tasting *mole* sauce, one that won't be forgotten.

You can find fresh and dried chili peppers in all Latin grocery stores and in many natural food stores, upscale markets, full-service grocery stores, and specialty food shops.

3 dried pasilla chilies, stemmed
3 dried ancho chilies, stemmed
3 dried chipotle chilies, stemmed
1 large onion, coarsely chopped
2 cloves garlic, coarsely chopped
4 medium tomatoes, coarsely chopped
2 teaspoons each ground cinnamon, cumin, and coriander
1 teaspoon each ground mace, cloves, and oregano
2 quarts water
3 vanilla pods, split lengthwise and beans removed
2 ounces bittersweet chocolate
3 tablespoons Vanilla Vinegar (page 22)
Salt and pepper, to taste
2 medium chickens (3½ pounds each), cut into serving pieces
2 tablespoons vegetable oil
½ cup coarsely chopped cilantro, for garnish

Place the chilies, onion, garlic, tomatoes, spices, oregano, water, two-thirds of the vanilla beans and three pods in a large, heavy-bottomed saucepan. Bring to a boil over high heat. Cook for 15 minutes, stirring frequently. Reduce the heat to moderately low and simmer for 1½ hours or until slightly thick and aromatic. Remove the vanilla pods and discard. Cool to room temperature.

Purée the mixture in a blender until fairly smooth, occasionally scraping down the sides of the container. Strain through a fine wire sieve and return to the saucepan. Add the chocolate, vanilla vinegar, and remaining vanilla beans and cook over moderate heat for 40 minutes, stirring occasionally. Season with salt and pepper and set aside until needed.

Preheat oven to 400°F.

In a large, nonstick sauté pan, brown the chicken in the vegetable oil in batches until golden brown on all sides. Transfer to a baking dish large enough to accommodate all the chicken in one layer. Pour the sauce over the chicken and cover with foil. Bake for 40 to 45 minutes or until the chicken is cooked through and the sauce is bubbling. Garnish with chopped cilantro and serve immediately.

Makes about 6 servings.

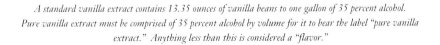

A standard vanilla extract contains 13.35 ounces of vanilla beans to one gallon of 35 percent alcohol. Pure vanilla extract must be comprised of 35 percent alcohol by volume for it to bear the label "pure vanilla extract." Anything less than this is considered a "flavor."

Glazed Carrots with Vanilla and Brown Sugar

These sweet-savory carrots are particularly good with smoked ham or turkey, but they would also be delicious with roast chicken or pork tenderloin.

1 small onion, cut into small dice
6 medium carrots, peeled and cut into ¾-inch pieces
3 tablespoons unsalted butter
2 cups dry white wine
2 tablespoons Vanilla Extract (page 18)
2 tablespoons light brown sugar
2 tablespoons Vanilla Vinegar (page 22)
Salt and pepper, to taste

In a large, heavy-bottomed sauté pan, sauté the onion and carrots in the butter over high heat for 3 minutes, stirring constantly. Add the wine and bring to a boil over high heat. Reduce the heat to moderately low and cook for 20 minutes or until the carrots are tender and the wine has evaporated. Add the vanilla extract, brown sugar, and vanilla vinegar. Cook over moderate heat for 3 to 4 minutes or until the carrots are coated with a medium-brown glaze. Season with salt and pepper and serve immediately.

Makes 4 servings.

To make a vanilla-scented potpourri, combine a handful of rose or other flower petals, orange peel, a few whole cloves, one or two sticks of cinnamon, and two tablespoons of vanilla extract. Mix well, transfer to an attractive bowl or vase, and enjoy the aroma.

Sweet Dishes

Banana and Vanilla Cream Pudding

This simple and easy recipe provides all the luscious flavors and textures of traditional banana cream pie, minus the crust. Serve this sweet pudding with a dollop of whipped cream and sugar cookies for a tempting dessert.

2 cups whole milk
2 vanilla pods, split lengthwise and beans removed
1 cup Vanilla Sugar (page 19)
6 egg yolks
½ teaspoon salt
½ cup all-purpose flour
1 tablespoon Vanilla Extract (page 18)
1 large ripe banana, peeled, halved, and cut into ¼-inch slices

Heat the milk and vanilla pods and beans in a large, heavy-bottomed saucepan over low heat until the liquid starts to simmer. Simmer for 3 minutes, stirring constantly. Remove the pods and discard.

Place the vanilla sugar, egg yolks, and salt in a large bowl; mix well. Sprinkle the flour over the surface of the sugar mixture and mix with a wooden spoon. Slowly add the hot milk mixture, whisking constantly until thoroughly incorporated. Return the mixture to the saucepan and cook over low heat, stirring constantly with a wire whisk, for 9 or 10 minutes or until the mixture is thick like pudding. (You may want to switch to a wooden spoon once the mixture is smooth and begins to thicken.) Add the vanilla extract, mix well, and remove from the heat. Cool to room temperature.

Add the banana, mix gently, and transfer to a bowl. Cover the surface with plastic wrap and refrigerate for 4 hours or up to 1 day before serving.

Makes about 4 servings.

Vanilla Pancakes with Dried Cherries

Serve these delectable, vanilla-laced pancakes with maple syrup or with Vanilla Syrup (page 21) for a real hit of vanilla. I adore pancakes and syrup served with some kind of smoked meat, preferably thick-sliced crispy bacon. If you cannot find dried cherries, substitute dried cranberries or raisins.

1 cup all-purpose flour
3 tablespoons cornmeal
2 tablespoons Vanilla Sugar (page 19)
1 teaspoon baking powder
½ teaspoon baking soda
½ teaspoon salt
1¼ cups buttermilk
1 vanilla pod, split lengthwise and beans removed
1 tablespoon Vanilla Extract (page 18)
1 egg, lightly beaten
2 tablespoons melted unsalted butter, cooled
1 cup coarsely chopped dried cherries
3 tablespoons vegetable oil, for cooking

In a large bowl, mix together the flour, cornmeal, vanilla sugar, baking powder, baking soda, and salt.

In a small bowl, whisk together the buttermilk, vanilla beans, vanilla extract, egg, melted butter, and dried cherries.

Make a small well in the center of the dry ingredients. Pour the wet ingredients into the dry and mix just until incorporated. (Overmixing will make the batter tough.) Refrigerate for 10 minutes.

Heat a large, nonstick skillet over moderate heat. Add 2 teaspoons of the vegetable oil. When the oil is hot but not smoking, spoon about 3 tablespoons batter for each pancake onto the skillet, allowing room for them to spread about 1 inch. Cook until the bottoms are light golden brown, 2 to 3 minutes. Flip and cook the opposite sides until they are light golden brown and the centers spring back when lightly pressed. Remove pancakes and keep warm in a low oven (200°F.) while you cook the remaining pancakes, adding oil to the pan as needed.

Makes about 12 pancakes.

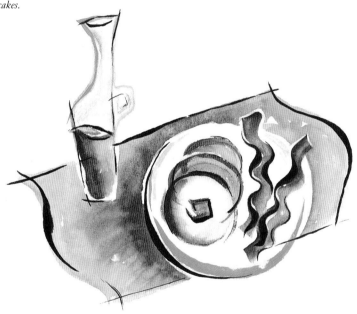

The average vanilla bean worker may hand-pollinate
anywhere from fifteen hundred to two thousand flowers in one day.

Vanilla Rice Pudding with Vanilla Sugar Crust

There aren't many dishes that match the comfort quotient of this heartwarming dessert. Nutmeg-scented sweet Asian rice and vanilla are a natural pair, and when cooked together, they form a flavorful and rich pudding. The browned-sugar crust adds a touch of elegance to this homey dessert.

2 vanilla pods, split lengthwise and beans removed
4 cups half-and-half
3 cups water
1 cup basmati rice
¾ teaspoon salt
¾ cup firmly packed light brown sugar
½ teaspoon ground nutmeg
½ cup golden raisins
1½ tablespoons Vanilla Extract (page 18)
½ cup Vanilla Sugar (see page 19)

Place the vanilla pods and beans, half-and-half, water, rice, salt, brown sugar, and nutmeg in a heavy-bottomed saucepan. Bring to a boil over high heat. Reduce the heat to moderately low and simmer 30 to 40 minutes, stirring occasionally. When the rice has absorbed most of the liquid and is tender, remove the vanilla pods and add the raisins and vanilla extract; mix well. Cook for 5 minutes, remove from heat, and cool to room temperature. Pour into a 6-cup, shallow, ovenproof baking dish, cover with plastic or foil, and refrigerate until cold and firm.

Preheat broiler for 15 minutes.

Remove the rice pudding from the refrigerator and sprinkle the vanilla sugar evenly over the surface. Place under the broiler for 5 to 7 minutes or until the vanilla sugar is golden brown and bubbling. Remove from the broiler and let sit at room temperature for 5 minutes. Spoon into individual bowls, distributing the sugar crust evenly; serve warm.

Makes 6 to 8 servings.

There are more than one hundred fifty organic chemicals that make up the flavor of the vanilla bean, but vanillin is responsible for about 30 percent of the flavor we know as vanilla.

Classic Crème Brûlée

It seems that almost every upscale restaurant menu now features a fancy version of *crème brûlée*. This recipe makes a pure and simple custard without the distraction of additional trendy flavoring agents. I use a small blowtorch to crystallize the sugar on my *crème brûlée*, but a preheated broiler also works just fine.

2 large eggs
3 egg yolks
⅔ cup granulated sugar
Pinch salt
1 tablespoon Vanilla Extract (page 18)
2½ cups heavy cream
2 vanilla pods, split lengthwise and beans removed
¼ cup lightly packed light brown sugar, sifted to remove lumps

Preheat oven to 350°F.

Place the whole eggs, egg yolks, granulated sugar, salt, and vanilla extract in a medium bowl. Mix until thoroughly combined.

Heat the cream and the vanilla beans in a heavy-bottomed saucepan over low heat for 7 to 10 minutes. Slowly add to the egg mixture, stirring gently as you go. (If you add the hot mixture too fast, the eggs will curdle.) Mix well and pour into four ¾-cup oven-proof ramekins.

Set the ramekins in a baking pan. Fill the pan with enough hot water to reach halfway up the sides of the ramekins. Bake for 25 to 30 minutes or until the custard is slightly firm to the touch. Remove from the oven and carefully lift the ramekins from the water bath. Cool to room temperature. Cover and refrigerate for at least 4 hours or preferably overnight.

Preheat broiler for 15 minutes.

Evenly sprinkle the surface of each custard with brown sugar. Place under the broiler until the sugar is melted, dark brown, and bubbling. Serve immediately if you like warm custard, or place in the refrigerator for 20 to 30 minutes if you prefer cool custard.

Makes 4 servings.

Deer's Tongue, also known as wild vanilla, grows in parts of North America.
The plant has an assertive vanilla odor and was used by early Native Americans
to scent tobacco and for medicinal purposes. Coumarin, a substance contained in Deer's Tongue,
was used as a flavoring agent in food until the mid 1950s, when it was banned by the
Food and Drug Administration. However, it is still used as the major flavoring compound
in inexpensive Mexican vanilla products.

Vanilla Cream Tartlets with Blueberries

Don't be put off by the long list of ingredients and directions—these irresistible tartlets are easy to prepare and assemble. The Vanilla Cream is even better the second day, and the pastry dough can be made one day ahead as well. If blueberries aren't in season, feel free to substitute any seasonal fresh fruit; fresh figs or other varieties of berries would be delicious.

Once the custard is placed in the baked shell, it's best to serve these desserts right away—the crust will become soggy if the custard sits inside for too long. You may however, bake the shells 1 to 2 days in advance, wrap in tin foil, and fill just before serving.

VANILLA CREAM:
2 cups whole milk
½ cup heavy cream
2 vanilla pods, split lengthwise and beans removed
¾ cup sugar
6 egg yolks
½ cup all-purpose flour
2 tablespoons unsalted butter

PASTRY:
1¼ cups all-purpose flour
¼ teaspoon salt
½ cup Vanilla Sugar (page 19)
4 ounces (1 stick) unsalted butter, cut into small pieces
½ large egg (see NOTE)
1 teaspoon Vanilla Extract (page 18)

2 cups blueberries
3 tablespoons Vanilla Syrup (page 21)

For the Vanilla Cream: Heat the milk, cream, and vanilla pods and beans in a heavy-bottomed saucepan over low heat until the liquid starts to simmer. Simmer for 3 minutes, stirring constantly. Remove the pods and discard.

Place the sugar and egg yolks in large bowl; mix well. Sprinkle the flour over the surface of the sugar mixture and mix with a wooden spoon. Slowly add the hot milk mixture, whisking constantly, until thoroughly incorporated. Return the mixture to the saucepan and cook over low heat, stirring constantly with a wire whisk, for 9 or 10 minutes or until the mixture is thick like pudding. (You may want to switch to a wooden spoon once the mixture is smooth and begins to thicken.) Add the butter and stir until melted.

Pour the mixture into a container and cool to room temperature. Cover the surface of the custard with plastic wrap and refrigerate for 4 hours or up to 2 days.

For the pastry: Preheat oven to 350°F. Butter six 4-inch tartlet tins. Place the flour, salt, and vanilla sugar in a medium bowl; mix well. Using your fingers, mix in the butter, one piece at a time, until the mixture resembles coarse meal. Mix the egg and vanilla extract together in a small bowl. Stir into the dry mixture and gather into a ball. Divide the dough into 6 flat discs and wrap each in plastic. Let dough stand at room temperature for 30 to 45 minutes. Place a disc in the center of each tartlet tin. Gently press the dough out to the edges, making a thin layer about ⅛ inch thick on the bottoms, and a double thickness of dough on the sides of the tins. (Let the dough come up over the edges about ¼ inch to allow for shrinkage.) Place on a baking sheet, cover with plastic, and refrigerate for about 1 hour or up to 1 day. Prick the bottoms of the dough several times with a fork. Bake on a sheet pan for 13 to 15 minutes or until they are light golden brown. Remove from the oven and cool to room temperature.

To assemble the tartlets: Spoon about 3 rounded tablespoons of the vanilla cream into each crust. In a bowl, combine the blueberries with the vanilla syrup and mix gently. Spoon some of the berries over the top of each custard, dividing equally, and serve immediately.

NOTE: To divide a whole egg, beat 1 egg lightly and divide in half (about 1½ tablespoons). Use only one half of the egg in the pastry or double the whole recipe to make 12 tartlets.

Makes six 4-inch tartlets.

To add an intriguing flavor to fresh lemonade, add a couple of teaspoons of vanilla extract
or the beans from several pods to the liquid; mix well and serve over ice.

Strawberries with Balsamic Vinegar and Vanilla

This Italian-inspired dessert takes only minutes to prepare. Sweet, tart, and sour, the balsamic vinegar intensifies both the color and flavor of sweet, ripe strawberries. Serve with biscotti or your favorite cookies and a sweet dessert wine for an elegant, light finish to a heavy or filling meal.

2 pints strawberries, stemmed and halved
1 vanilla pod, split lengthwise and beans removed
2 tablespoons Vanilla Sugar (page 19)
3 tablespoons balsamic vinegar

Place the strawberries in a bowl. Mix the vanilla beans, vanilla sugar, and balsamic vinegar in a small bowl. Add to the strawberries and mix gently. Macerate at room temperature for 1 hour or in the refrigerator for up to 6 hours. Serve slightly chilled or at room temperature.

Makes 4 servings.

During Prohibition it wasn't uncommon for alcoholics to drink vanilla extract as a substitute for unavailable distilled spirits such as whiskey or scotch. Although vanilla extract contains only 35 percent alcohol, at the time a little alcohol was considered better than none at all.

Vanilla Bars with Pecans and Coconut

It used to be hard for me to imagine a brownie worth eating if it wasn't packed full of chocolate, but these blond brownies have taken first place on my list of favorite desserts. Both the rolled oats and the coconut ensure moist, chewy bars.

8 ounces (2 sticks) unsalted butter, melted
2 vanilla pods, split lengthwise and beans removed
2 cups firmly packed light brown sugar
2 large eggs
2 tablespoons Vanilla Extract (page 18)
1½ cups all-purpose flour
¾ teaspoon baking powder
¼ teaspoon salt
1 cup rolled oats
1 cup chopped toasted pecans
¾ cup shredded coconut

Preheat oven to 325°F. Lightly grease and flour a 9-x-13-inch baking pan.

In a large bowl, mix together the butter, vanilla beans, and sugar. Add the eggs and vanilla extract and beat for 3 minutes. Add the flour, baking powder, and salt and mix well. Add the oats, pecans, and coconut and mix just until thoroughly incorporated.

Pour into the prepared pan and bake on the lower rack of the oven for 15 minutes. Rotate to the upper rack and bake an additional 20 to 25 minutes or until a toothpick inserted in the center comes out clean. Remove from the oven and cool to room temperature before cutting. Cut into rectangles to serve.

Makes about 15 brownies.

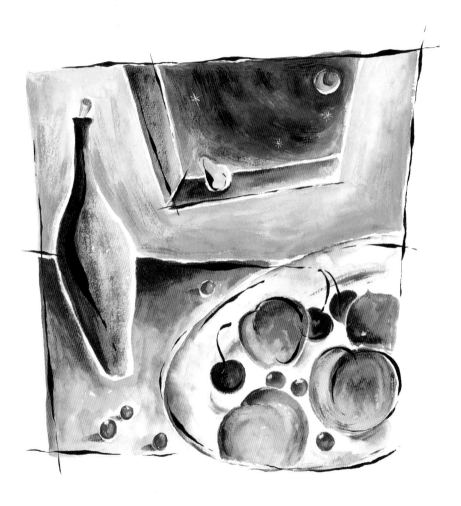

Poached Summer Fruits with Vanilla

This refreshing fruit dessert takes less than twenty minutes to make and can be served warm over ice cream, with pound cake, or on its own in an attractive bowl. It is also delicious served chilled and garnished with vanilla yogurt or, for a richer dessert, whipped cream spiked with a fruit liqueur.

Peaches, nectarines, blackberries, and plums can also be used in this recipe, but I adore this particular combination of red-, blue-, and orange-colored summer fruits.

One 750 ml bottle white dessert wine (Essensia or late-harvest Riesling)
2 vanilla pods, split lengthwise and beans removed
2 cups pitted cherries
1 cup blueberries
8 small firm apricots, halved and pits removed

Place the wine and vanilla pods and beans in a heavy-bottomed saucepan. Bring to a boil over high heat and cook for 10 minutes.

Add the cherries, blueberries, and apricots and return to a boil. Reduce the heat to low and simmer until the fruit is tender but not mushy, 3 to 5 minutes. Remove the vanilla pods and discard. Spoon the fruit into shallow bowls along with some of the poaching liquid.

Makes about 4 servings.

To add an intriguing flavor to fresh lemonade, add a couple of teaspoons of vanilla extract or the beans from several pods to the liquid; mix well and serve over ice.

White Chocolate and Vanilla Cake

This moist yellow cake is so rich and buttery it doesn't even need icing. The cake naturally sinks in the center, but don't worry; it doesn't affect the flavor or texture. You may serve wedges of the cake unadorned for breakfast or a snack; or dusted with powdered sugar, dolloped with whipped cream, or topped with fresh fruit for a satisfying dessert.

6 ounces white chocolate
8 ounces (2 sticks) unsalted butter
2 vanilla pods, split lengthwise and beans removed
1 tablespoon Vanilla Extract (page 18)
2 cups sifted all-purpose flour
2 cups Vanilla Sugar (page 19)
1½ teaspoons baking powder
1 teaspoon baking soda
1 teaspoon salt
1 cup milk
4 large eggs

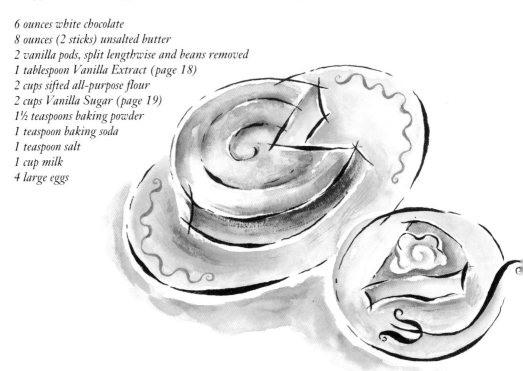

Preheat oven to 350°F. Lightly grease two 8-inch round cake pans and line the bottom of each pan with parchment paper. Lightly butter the parchment paper.

Melt the chocolate and butter with the vanilla beans in the top of a double boiler over simmering water; stir in the vanilla extract. Cool to room temperature and set aside until needed.

Mix the flour, vanilla sugar, baking powder, baking soda, and salt together in a large bowl. Add the chocolate mixture, milk, and eggs and beat until smooth. Spread into the prepared pans and bake in the center of the oven for 35 to 40 minutes or until the tops are golden brown and the cakes spring back when gently poked with a finger. Remove from the oven and cool in the pans for 45 minutes. Run a dull knife around the edge of each cake and gently turn out each onto a flat plate. Slice into wedges and serve warm or at room temperature.

Makes two 8-inch cakes.

Vanilla-Pecan Shortbread

I've found that shortbread can be addictive. These shortbread cookies, accented with vanilla beans and studded with toasted pecans, are sure to test your willpower. Serve this golden brown, triangle-shaped shortbread with ice cream or pudding, or with brandy, espresso, or after-dinner drinks for an elegant, uncomplicated dessert.

6 ounces (1½ sticks) unsalted butter, softened
½ cup firmly packed light brown sugar
2 vanilla pods, split lengthwise and beans removed
2 teaspoons Vanilla Extract (page 18)
1½ cups all-purpose flour
¼ cup cornstarch, sifted
¼ teaspoon salt
½ cup coarsely chopped toasted pecans

Preheat oven to 325°F. Lightly butter a 10-inch glass pie pan.

Place the butter in a medium bowl and beat with an electric mixer until smooth and pale yellow. Add the sugar, vanilla beans, and vanilla extract and beat on high speed for 3 to 4 minutes until light and fluffy. Add the flour, cornstarch, salt, and pecans and mix well. Gather the dough into a ball.

Press the dough into the bottom of the prepared pie pan, building edges ½ inch up the sides of the pan. Cut into 12 wedges, cutting all the way through the dough. Pierce each wedge in three places with a fork. Bake for 40 minutes or until light brown. Remove from oven, recut wedges, and cool in pan to room temperature. Serve immediately, or store tightly wrapped in plastic or foil at room temperature for up to 5 days.

Makes 12 wedges.

Vanilla-Plum Sorbet

Vanilla is a natural flavor companion to juicy, ripe plums and sweet strawberries. This refreshing, deep ruby–colored sorbet can be served as a refresher between courses or as a dessert, along with cookies and after-dinner drinks.

8 large ripe plums, pitted and coarsely chopped
½ pint strawberries, stemmed and coarsely chopped
¼ cup water
3 vanilla pods, split lengthwise and beans removed
½ cup Vanilla Sugar (page 19)
Mint sprigs, for garnish

Place the plums, strawberries, water, and vanilla pods and beans in a 4-quart, heavy-bottomed saucepan. Bring to a boil over high heat, stirring constantly. Reduce the heat to moderate and cook for 25 to 30 minutes or until the fruit has broken down and the mixture is thick. Remove the pods and cool the fruit mixture to room temperature.

Purée the fruit in a blender until smooth. Strain the mixture through a fine wire sieve, pushing the pulp through to extract as much juice as possible. Return the strained mixture to the saucepan and add the vanilla sugar. Bring to a boil over moderately high heat, stirring constantly to prevent the mixture from sticking. Cook for 5 minutes, stirring constantly. Transfer to a nonreactive container and cool to room temperature.

When cool, cover with a tight-fitting lid or tin foil and freeze for 8 hours or overnight before serving. When firm, serve in small glasses, garnished with sprigs of mint.

Makes 4 to 6 servings.

White Chocolate and Vanilla Mousse

What could be better than a rich, dark chocolate mousse? Velvety white chocolate mousse scented with plenty of vanilla! This confection is definitely for those who enjoy wicked and decadent desserts with lots of flavor and a creamy texture. At first glance the directions may appear complicated, but once you start preparing this recipe you'll see how simple it is to make.

4 ounces white chocolate
4 ounces (1 stick) unsalted butter
2 tablespoons Vanilla Extract (page 18)
3 large eggs, separated
¾ cup Vanilla Sugar (page 19)
3 tablespoons cold water
½ cup heavy cream

In the top of a double boiler, heat the chocolate and butter over simmering water until melted. Add the vanilla extract and mix well. Cool to room temperature and set aside until needed.

In a medium bowl, beat the egg yolks until thickened and lemon-colored, about 4 minutes.

Heat the vanilla sugar and cold water in a small saucepan over low heat until the mixture begins to boil. Gradually pour into the egg yolks, beating constantly.

Place the egg yolk mixture in the top of a double boiler over almost boiling water. Using a wire whisk, beat the mixture for 5 minutes or until doubled in volume. Remove from the hot water and beat another 5 minutes. Fold the chocolate mixture into the egg yolk mixture and mix gently.

In a small bowl, beat the egg whites until stiff but not dry. Fold the whites into the chocolate mixture and mix gently. Beat the cream until stiff; fold into the chocolate mixture and mix gently. Transfer to a bowl, cover with plastic wrap, and refrigerate for 8 hours or overnight before serving. Spoon into dessert dishes and serve chilled.

Makes about 4 servings.

The European species of oak commonly used to make wine casks (Quercus robur and Quercus sessilis) leaks small amounts of vanillin into the wines, thus imparting that familiar vanilla flavor often associated with barrel-aged wines.

Vanilla Caramel Cream Sauce

Definitely not a low-calorie dessert sauce, make this luxurious concoction when you're in the mood to pamper yourself. Pour the creamy sauce over vanilla ice cream or drizzle over a walnut tart or pound cake.

3 cups water
2 cups Vanilla Sugar (page 19)
4 vanilla pods, split lengthwise and beans removed
1 cup heavy cream
4 ounces (1 stick) unsalted butter, cut into 8 pieces
Pinch salt

Place the water, vanilla sugar, and vanilla pods in a 4-quart, heavy-bottomed saucepan. Bring to a boil over high heat. Cook over high heat for 15 to 20 minutes, stirring frequently, until the mixture is dark brown, thick, and syrupy. Remove from the heat and cool slightly. Remove and discard the pods.

Add the cream (the mixture will sputter when you add the cream, so step back at first and then be prepared to stir the mixture vigorously). When the cream has been absorbed, add the butter and the salt and cook over moderately low heat until the butter has melted and the mixture is smooth. Serve warm.

The sauce can be stored in a covered container in the refrigerator for up to 3 weeks. To reheat the sauce, place in a heavy-bottomed saucepan and add a little milk or half-and-half. Heat over low heat, stirring frequently, until soft and pourable.

Makes about 2 cups.

Vanilla-Orange-Black Pepper Granité

The flavor combination of vanilla and orange reminds me of one of my favorite childhood treats—Creamsicles. This contemporary, more sophisticated recipe uses vanilla and orange as the primary flavors, but a hint of black pepper and finely crushed ice, rather than cream, make this sweet, cooling dessert refreshing and unique.

2 cups water
1 cup fresh orange juice
2 cups Vanilla Sugar (page 19)
4 vanilla pods, split lengthwise and beans removed
2 teaspoons coarsely cracked black peppercorns
2 tablespoons Vanilla Extract (page 18)
8 ice cubes, coarsely crushed

Place the water, orange juice, vanilla sugar, vanilla pods and beans, and black peppercorns in a 4-quart, heavy-bottomed saucepan. Bring to a boil over high heat. Cook over high heat for 15 minutes, stirring frequently and scraping the sides of the pan, until thick and syrupy. Add the vanilla extract and mix well. Strain into a nonreactive metal container, cover, and place in the freezer overnight or up to 2 months. (The mixture won't freeze but it will become slushy and icy.)

Place the ice cubes in a blender along with the vanilla-orange mixture. Blend until the ice is finely crushed and mixture is well blended. Spoon into shallow serving cups or glasses and serve immediately.

Makes 4 to 6 servings.

Vanilla Bavarian Cream with Pistachios

Elegant and heady with the fragrance of vanilla, this attractive dessert makes a dramatic presentation and an excellent finale to a lavish meal. You may also serve this molded dessert with a mélange of mixed summer berries or fresh figs macerated in port wine.

2 envelopes gelatin (about 5 teaspoons)
⅓ cup cold water
1⅓ cups Vanilla Sugar (page 19)
6 large egg yolks
1 cup whole milk
1¼ cups heavy cream
2 vanilla pods, split lengthwise and beans removed
1 cup coarsely chopped toasted pistachios

Soak the gelatin in the cold water (rub with your fingers to dissolve the grains) for 15 minutes.

Meanwhile, in a large bowl, combine 1 cup of the vanilla sugar and the egg yolks and beat until pale yellow in color, about 3 minutes.

Place the milk, ¼ cup of the heavy cream, and the vanilla beans in a heavy-bottomed saucepan. Heat over moderate heat just until it begins to boil. Add the milk mixture a little at a time to the sugar and eggs, whisking constantly. Return the mixture to the saucepan and heat over moderate heat, stirring constantly, until thick, about 7 or 8 minutes. (Do not let the mixture boil or the eggs will curdle.) Add the gelatin to the mixture and beat with a wire whisk to incorporate. Remove from the heat and strain through a fine wire sieve. Cool to room temperature.

In a small bowl, beat the remaining 1 cup heavy cream with the remaining ⅓ cup vanilla sugar until it forms stiff peaks. Gently fold into the custard mixture and mix well. Turn the custard into an 8-cup fluted mold and cover the surface with plastic wrap. Refrigerate for 8 hours or overnight before serving.

To serve, set the mold in a larger pan filled with hot water for 2 minutes. Run a dull knife around the edges of the custard to help unmold. Place a large plate over the top of the mold. Quickly flip the plate and mold over, keeping the plate firmly against the mold. The custard will unmold onto the plate. Slice into wedges for serving. Alternatively, slice the custard in the pan and serve on individual plates. Garnish with the pistachios and serve immediately.

Makes about 8 servings.

The intense flavor of chocolate is comprised in part by the addition of a healthy dose of vanilla. It may be difficult to discern the flavor of vanilla, but chocolate devoid of it would be flat and one-dimensional.

Vanilla-Mango Freeze

Light, low-fat, and healthful, this vanilla-spiked tropical fruit concoction is sure to be a favorite with those watching their calorie and fat intake. This pleasing dessert takes only a few minutes to prepare and can be stored in the freezer for up to two weeks.

3 ripe mangoes, peeled, pits removed, coarsely chopped (about 2½ cups)
2 vanilla pods, split lengthwise and beans removed
¾ cup nonfat vanilla yogurt
Dash each nutmeg and salt
Mint sprigs, for garnish

Place the mango and vanilla beans in a blender. Purée until smooth, occasionally scraping down the sides of the container. Strain through a fine wire sieve, pushing the pulp and juice through to extract as much fruit as possible.

Transfer to a stainless steel or plastic bowl and add the yogurt, nutmeg, and salt; mix well. Cover tightly and freeze for 8 hours or overnight. Serve in small bowls, garnished with sprigs of mint.

Makes about 4 servings.

To give your bath water a vanilla scent, add two or three tablespoons
of vanilla extract just before slipping into the hot water.

Vanilla-White Chocolate Sauce

This sinful dessert sauce is delicious drizzled over fruit-flavored or chocolate ice cream, simple, unadorned cakes, or fresh fruit. When refrigerated for a couple of days, this sauce hardens and becomes the perfect filling for chocolate cookies—for those of us who love Oreos.

2 cups heavy cream
2 vanilla pods, split lengthwise and beans removed
2 tablespoons unsalted butter
3 ounces white chocolate, coarsely chopped
1 tablespoon Vanilla Extract (page 18)

Place the heavy cream, vanilla pods, and beans in a heavy-bottomed saucepan. Bring to a boil over high heat, stirring constantly to prevent the cream from boiling over. Reduce the heat to moderately high and cook, stirring constantly, for 15 to 17 minutes or until the cream has reduced by one half. Remove the vanilla pods and discard.

Add the butter and chocolate and cook over low heat until melted, about 5 minutes. Add the vanilla extract and mix well. Serve warm or at cool room temperature. To store, cover tightly and refrigerate for up to 2 weeks. Reheat gently to ensure easy pouring.

Makes about 1½ cups.

Table of Equivalents

The exact equivalents in the following tables have been rounded for convenience.

US/UK

oz=ounce
lb=pound
in=inch
ft=foot
tbl=tablespoon
fl oz=fluid ounce
qt=quart

Metric

g=gram
kg=kilogram
mm=millimeter
cm=centimeter
ml=milliliter
l=liter

Liquids

US	Metric	UK
2 tbl	30 ml	1 fl oz
½ cup	60 ml	2 fl oz
⅓ cup	80 ml	3 fl oz
½ cup	125 ml	4 fl oz
⅔ cup	160 ml	5 fl oz
¾ cup	180 ml	6 fl oz
1 cup	250 ml	8 fl oz
1½ cups	375 ml	12 fl oz
2 cups	500 ml	16 fl oz
4 cups/1 qt	1 l	32 fl oz

Weights

US/UK	Metric
1 oz	30 g
2 oz	60 g
3 oz	90 g
4 oz (¼ lb)	125 g
5 oz (⅓ lb)	155 g
6 oz	185 g
7 oz	220 g
8 oz (½ lb)	250 g
10 oz	315 g
12 oz (¾ lb)	375 g
14 oz	440 g
16 oz (1 lb)	500 g
1½ lb	750 g
2 lb	1 kg
3 lb	1.5 kg

Table of Equivalents

The exact equivalents in the following tables have been rounded for convenience.

Oven Temperatures

Fahrenheit	Celsius	Gas
250	120	½
275	140	1
300	150	2
325	160	3
350	180	4
375	190	5
400	200	6
425	220	7
450	230	8
475	240	9
500	260	10

Length Measures

⅛ in	3 mm
¼ in	6 mm
½ in	12 mm
1 in	2.5 cm
2 in	5 cm
3 in	7.5 cm
4 in	10 cm
5 in	13 cm
6 in	15 cm
7 in	18 cm
8 in	20 cm
9 in	23 cm
10 in	25 cm
11 in	28 cm
12 in/1 ft	30 cm

Index